Natural Disasters

Ferocious Fires

Julie Richards

This edition first published in 2002 in the United States of America by Chelsea House Publishers, a subsidiary of Haights Cross Communications.

Reprinted 2002

Chelsea House Publishers
1974 Sproul Road, Suite 400
Broomall, PA 19008-0914

The Chelsea House world wide web address is www.chelseahouse.com

Library of Congress Cataloging-in-Publication Data Applied for.

ISBN 0-7910-6583-9

First published in 2001 by
Macmillan Education Australia Pty Ltd
627 Chapel Street, South Yarra, Australia 3141

Copyright © Julie Richards 2001

Edited by Sally Woollett
Text design by Polar Design Pty Ltd
Cover design by Polar Design Pty Ltd
Illustrations and maps by Pat Kermode, Purple Rabbit Productions
Printed in Hong Kong

Acknowledgements
The author and the publisher are grateful to the following for permission to reproduce copyright material:

Cover photograph: Fire burning fiercely, courtesy of Photolibrary.com.

AP/AAP, p. 8 (bottom); Australian Picture Library/CORBIS, pp. 6, 7, 11 (top), 16, 17; Australian Picture Library/Leo Meier, p. 18; Australian Picture Library/Pacific Stock, p. 14 (bottom); Australian Picture Library/W. Herzfeld, p. 21; CFA, pp. 8 (top), 14 (top), 22–23, 23 (bottom), 24, 25; Coo-ee Picture Library, pp. 22 (bottom), 28 (both); CSIRO, pp. 11 (bottom), 29; CSIRO Australia 2000— image reproduced with permission of CSIRO Forestry and Forestry Products, Canberra Australia, p. 15 (top); Forestry SA 2000, p. 4; PhotoDisc, pp. 2, 3, 15 (bottom), 19, 20, 31, 32; Photolibrary.com, p. 12; Reuters/Rick Wilking, p. 27.

While every care has been taken to trace and acknowledge copyright the publishers tender their apologies for any accidental infringement where copyright has proved untraceable. Where the attempt has been unsuccessful, the publisher welcomes information that would redress the situation.

Contents

An orange tongue of flame

It is a very hot summer. Thick forests and tall grasslands are so dry they crackle. Great summer thunderstorms have formed and lightning leaps from cloud to cloud.

Suddenly, a ribbon of **lightning** jumps from the storm and zig-zags towards the ground. With a **splintering crack** it strikes the top of a dead tree, splitting the trunk and slicing off branches in a **shower of sparks**. Splinters of smoking wood **glow brightly**.

The glowing splinters drift down to the forest floor.

Within minutes, a small, **orange tongue** of flame peeks above the twigs and leaves and licks at nearby plants.

Before long, **fire** races through the forest once again, changing the landscape just as it has done for millions of years.

FIRE is nature's way of cleaning up the forest. Clearing away dead and sick trees and plants renews the forest environment. Sometimes the fire spreads beyond the forest and nobody can stop it. When a forest fire threatens homes and lives it becomes a natural disaster.

What is fire?

Fire happens when something is heated until it becomes so hot that a special type of **reaction** happens. This reaction makes a burst of heat and light. This is called **ignition point**, which we see as a flame. When heat changes the shape or state of something in this way it is called combustion.

The fire triangle

Three things are needed to start a fire: oxygen, fuel and heat. This is called the **fire triangle**. Take away one of these things and a fire cannot start.

Oxygen

Oxygen is in the air we breathe. A fire sucks the oxygen from the air around it. The oxygen mixes with the burning material and keeps the fire burning. The more oxygen there is, the bigger and more fierce the fire can become.

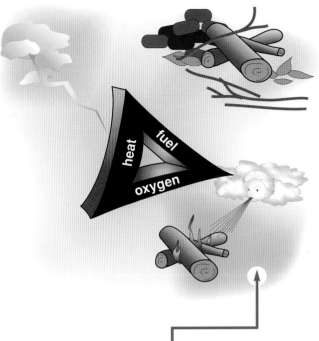

The fire triangle. A fire only goes out when combustion stops. Combustion only stops if one of the parts of a fire triangle is taken away.

 GUESS WHAT?

The Earth's atmosphere has just the right amount of oxygen for fire. The Moon has no atmosphere at all. Planets such as Venus may have an atmosphere, but they contain no oxygen. These are worlds without fire.

Fuel

Anything that burns is fuel. Wood, grass, paper, oil, petrol and coal are all examples of fuel. Some burn faster than others. A dried out dead tree burns much quicker than a young tree still green with life and filled with water.

Heat

Heat dries up any water inside the fuel. A lightning bolt is five times hotter than the surface of the Sun, so even though a lightning bolt may only touch the ground for a moment, there is enough heat to set the fuel alight.

A controlled burn is lit to remove dry fuel.

Wildfires

Sometimes a fire is lit to clear the land of undergrowth and trees so that there is less fuel for a wildfire to burn or so cattle can graze. This sort of fire is called a controlled burn. At all times, the fire is watched very closely and never allowed to become a danger to people. A fire that is not controlled is called a wildfire.

Sometimes, even controlled burns can lead to disaster. In 1989, seven firefighters were killed in Canada by a wildfire that had been lit as a controlled fire only ten minutes before.

 Disaster Detective

For over 50,000 years, **indigenous peoples** have used fire to clear the land. See if you can find out why they did this and how it helped them to hunt and survive.

When do wildfires happen?

The time of the year when wildfires are likely to happen is called fire season or the fire danger period. Fire season changes from year to year and from place to place—it begins whenever there is the chance of wildfires starting. Two very important things are considered before a decision is made to declare the start of fire season.

Weather

Sizzling temperatures and hot, dry winds quickly drive any moisture from fuel. High winds mean that there is plenty of oxygen to feed a fire and push it along. Lightning strikes provide heat. Heat can also come from a dropped cigarette, a campfire that has not been properly put out or sparks from faulty power lines.

GUESS WHAT?

At any given moment there are between 1,800 and 2,000 thunderstorms happening around the world. A single lightning bolt carries enough electricity to power a light bulb for three months! Lightning once started 1,400 fires in ten days.

Forests contain a lot of fuel for a fire.

Fuel

The amount of **vegetation** is also very important. Spring is usually warm and wet. This encourages plants and trees to grow very quickly. By the time summer arrives, there is plenty of fuel ready to dry out and burn.

Where do wildfires happen?

A grassfire can race along at 65 kilometers (40 miles) per hour.

Wildfires can happen in any area where there are a lot of plants and grasses. Even if the vegetation is patchy, if there has been little or no rain for some time, then everything will be so dry that not much heating will be needed to make it burn.

Wildfires can rage through mountains or across flat, open plains. A grassfire begins in land where trees are few and tall grasses **thrive**. Scrub fires usually burn in areas covered in shrubs and small trees.

What about rainforests?

Lightning is the biggest cause of natural wildfire on the Earth. Dense rainforests and ice-covered lands are the only parts of our planet that have not been naturally shaped by fire. Although rainforests have plenty of fuel and lightning, the wet weather cools the heat so the fuel never properly dries out. Even a lightning bolt cannot trigger a fire here.

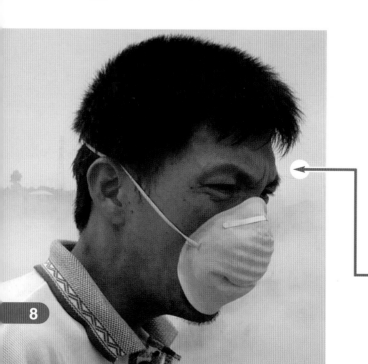

Forest fires burned out of control in Indonesia during 1997 and 1998. For many months, smoke blocked out the sun, closed airports and made people ill.

Read All About It!

Fire Rages in Rainforest

In 1997 and 1998, native rainforest in Indonesia was cleared by lighting fires. The fires raced out of control and could not be put out. The **monsoon** rains were late and the fires continued to burn for four months. Much of South-East Asia was covered by a thick cloud of smoke. Many people found it difficult to breathe. Airports had to be closed because it was too dangerous for aircraft to fly through the smoke.

How does a fire start?

Preheating

A fire will not start until the fuel is hot enough to ignite. The time when the fuel is heating up is called **preheating**. The heat can travel to the fuel and warm it in three different ways.

Radiation

If you stand in the sun or near another source of heat you can feel the heat warming your skin. This is because the heat is moving in rays or waves. This movement of heat away from its source is known as **radiation**. Once a wildfire is burning, waves of heat can dry and warm nearby plants in the same way. When the vegetation becomes hot enough, it too will burst into flames. This keeps the fire burning.

Convection

As well as moving by radiation, hot air will also move about by a process called **convection**. When air is warmed it becomes lighter and rises above the cooler air. The cooler air fills the space the rising air leaves behind. When the cooler air is heated, it rises and is replaced by more cool air. The movement of all this hot air can heat fuel to its ignition point.

Heat can warm fuel by radiation and convection.

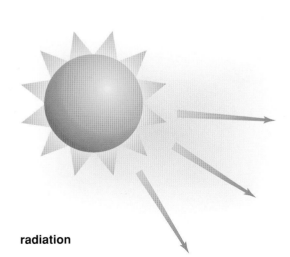

radiation

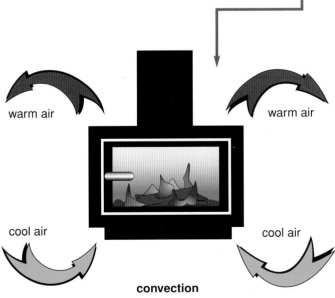

warm air
warm air

cool air
cool air

convection

Conduction

If you have ever touched the handle of a metal teaspoon left standing in a hot drink, you will have noticed how warm it felt. This is because the metal is a material that allows heat to move through it easily. The movement of heat in this way is called **conduction**, and an object that carries the heat is a conductor of heat.

Fires are not usually started by conduction, but fuel can be preheated by heat conducted from a fire that is already burning fiercely.

Not all fuels catch fire at the same time. If a lighted match is held against a thin sheet of paper and a twig, which do you think will burn first? The thinner paper will take far less time to preheat than the twig.

conduction

The metal teaspoon in this hot drink acts as a conductor of heat.

GUESS WHAT?

A fire can create weather! Large fires create their own weather by **superheating** the air around them. When this hot air rises, cool air rushes in to fill the empty space. This oxygen-rich air feeds the fire, making it hotter and stronger. All this rising hot air and rushing wind can build thunderclouds high above the fire. More lightning can come from these clouds to start new fires. Sometimes, heavy rain follows, putting the fire out.

Types of wildfire

Ground fire

A layer of dead leaves and grass covers the forest floor. When a fire burns beneath this layer it is called a ground fire. Most ground fires burn very slowly and usually go out by themselves, because the fuel is too cool and damp for flames to take over.

Surface fire

If the layer of fuel on the surface of the ground is very dry, a ground fire can break through it, burning grass, shrubs, broken branches and even small trees. When this happens, flames appear and the ground fire becomes a surface fire.

A surface fire spreads across the forest floor, gobbling up the plants and brush close to the ground. This part of the forest is called the **understory**. By burning the understory, a fire clears out dead wood, making room for new plants and trees to grow. Most tall trees are untouched by surface fires.

Ground fires burn slowly beneath the layer of dead leaves on the forest floor.

A surface fire burns the plants at the bottom of these trees.

Crown fire

Sometimes the understory has not burned for many years and the forest floor may be piled high with tangled plants and creepers. Large branches might be resting against small trees. A surface fire can use these branches as a ladder to climb into the taller trees. When a wildfire rages through the treetops, or forest **canopy**, it becomes a **crown fire**. A crown fire is the most destructive and powerful of all forest wildfires.

Firestorm

Firestorms are very **intense** fires that produce strong winds. These winds are created by the process of convection that you learned about earlier. The winds carry the heat of the fire, which ignites any fuel in its path. Firestorms can give out as much energy in 15 minutes as a nuclear explosion!

Fast-moving crown fires can leap from treetop to treetop.

GUESS WHAT?

Did you know that trees can explode? Deep inside the trunks of trees water travels between the roots and the leaves. A firestorm can heat the water until it boils into steam and bursts through the bark.

Fire devil

During a wildfire, the intense heat of the flames pulls in very strong gusts of wind. The hot air spirals upwards, drawing the flames into a twisting column called a fire devil. Although this fiery whirlwind is only short lived, it is still able to rip small trees from the ground and toss burning branches aside as it moves through.

Fireballs

A fireball is a burning bubble of gas. In a forest of eucalypt trees, the tops of the trees can burn very, very fast—within three to four seconds. The intense heat can make chemicals inside the leaves change into gas. As the gas becomes hot, it rises into the air above the treetops, floating like a ball of flame.

Read All About It!

Reporter Sees His Own House Burn

Radio journalist Murray Nichol was reporting live from the 1983 Ash Wednesday fires in the Adelaide Hills, Australia. As he described the homes burning beneath the helicopter, he realized that one of them was actually his own home.

A fire devil is a burning spiral of hot air.

Life cycle of a wildfire

Flaming combustion

When fuel bursts into flames it is called flaming combustion. The fire will be at its hottest during this time. The burning edge of the fire is called the **flaming front**. The flaming front will preheat surrounding plants and grass by radiation and convection until they too catch fire. This is how a hungry fire moves through the forest, swallowing everything in its path.

The wildfire's journey

Where the wildfire travels and how fast it goes depends on:

➤ the speed and direction of the wind

➤ the weather

➤ fuel

➤ the shape of the land.

During the daytime, fires burn fiercely because the wind and temperature rise in the afternoon. At night, when the wind and temperature usually drop, fires slow down.

When hot air rises it can dry out and preheat fuel on a hillside, allowing the fire to travel upwards. Narrow gullies can be especially dangerous because lots of air is being forced through a very tight space, making the wind blow even faster. These flames will be speedier than the rest of the fire.

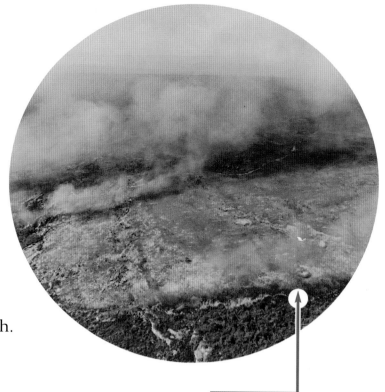

The yellow-orange line of flames is called the flaming front.

Wind can push a fire uphill.

These spot fires were started when the wind carried hot embers away from the main fire.

Natural barriers

Rivers, cliffs and steep rock faces can act as barriers and stop a fire from going any further. However, if the wind suddenly begins to blow from another direction, the fire can strengthen and move over fresh ground away from a barrier.

Spot fires

Strong winds can carry glowing **embers** up into the air. When the embers fall back to earth they can start new fires wherever they land. These are called spot fires. Firefighters have to keep watch because spot fires can begin burning around or behind them, and they can become trapped.

Glowing combustion

Once the line of flames has passed it might look as if the fire has gone. This is not so. The fuel is still burning, but it burns in a different way now. It burns very slowly by **glowing combustion**. It will keep burning this way for days or even weeks until the fuel is used up, rain falls or somebody puts it out.

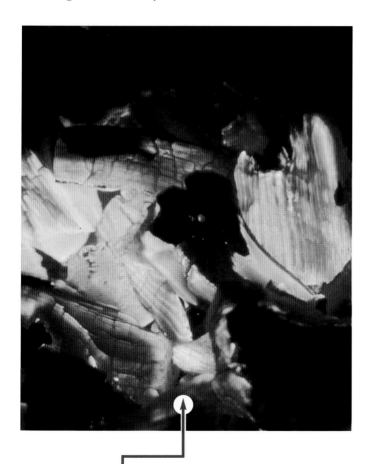

Glowing combustion.

What happens in the forest after a wildfire?

Fire changes the land. Much of the forest is left blackened and smoking. Once thickly knotted with plants, the ground is now **charred** and bare. Sunlight streams into the forest now that the leaves are gone from the branches.

It is silent. There are no birds or animals. Do you think this will make a difference to the forest? Perhaps you think the forest is dead and gone forever. You will be surprised at what happens in a forest after a wildfire. Wildfires can be very good for them.

Looking at this burnt forest, it is hard to see how wildfires can be good for it.

Growing back

Each type of plant, animal and insect has its own special way of surviving a wildfire.

 Disaster Detective

Giant redwood trees that grow in California, in the USA, are the largest living things on Earth! Their bark is so thick they can survive most fires and live for hundreds of years. Some types of eucalypt forests can release up to 14 million seeds over a very small area. Perhaps you can find out if there are other plants and trees that have their own special way of surviving a fire.

Fireweed appears soon after a wildfire. Its roots soak up the goodness from the ash in the soil before the soil is washed away by rain. As the plant dies, it returns this goodness to the soil.

Plants

Almost straight away, a green cover will appear on the forest floor. The extra sunlight means that many new plants can grow—plants that would not survive with the forest canopy blocking the light.

The flames have cleared all the dead and sick trees away. Soon, new trees will be growing in their place. The ash left behind is full of minerals that soak into the soil. These minerals are like vitamins to plants and trees! They can use them to grow strong and healthy.

Some pine trees, banksias and eucalypts have special seed cones that will only open when the extreme heat of a fire makes them pop. Even if the tree is destroyed, fresh young trees will soon sprout beside it.

Animals

Many animals are driven from the forest by the wildfire. Small animals such as mice and rabbits may leave smoke-filled burrows. Hawks and other birds of prey often hover at the wildfire's edge, ready to swoop onto these creatures as they try to escape the flames.

The trees and plants that provided homes or food for animals may be gone. That does not mean that there will be no animals. Instead, new animals will come to nest and eat the different vegetation that starts to grow back.

Big animals that would have found the cluttered forest floor too difficult to move around in will enjoy the space the wildfire has left behind. Animals that relied on the undergrowth for protection will need to go elsewhere before **predators** eat them. With fewer trees and extra sunlight, juicy grasses will grow tall. Grazing animals will come to feed on them.

Some animals will only nest in hollow trees. It may be some years after a wildfire before they return to the forest.

Birds

Birds that nested in the hollows of trees will not return to nest in the forest for some time after a wildfire. Neither will insect-eating birds—it will take between three and five years for the ground cover in which the insects live to build up again. However, other birds that like this new forest will nest in the trees left standing. They will feed on the nectar as the new plants begin to flower soon after the fire.

Damage

Although wildfires help forests to survive and stay healthy, some changes are so big that it will be many years before everything returns to normal.

If too many trees die

Beneath the ground, the roots of trees, shrubs and grass weave together like a giant net. This net holds the soil in its place. Without it, the soil would be washed into creeks and rivers when it rained, or it would be blown away by winds. Big trees would fall over because there would be nothing to hold them up. When the soil crumbles away, all the goodness goes with it, leaving the plants and trees to starve.

If heavy rain comes after the wildfire

In heavy rain, all the water can mix with ash, soil and charred wood. It can pour downhill as a mudslide, blocking up rivers and streams and killing fish and insects. The animals that depended on the insects or fish for food will have to find a new place to live.

If heavy rains come soon after a wildfire, charred wood, ash and soil can wash into rivers, streams and lakes.

Read All About It!

Flooding Rains Put Out Wildfire in Yellowstone National Park

In Yellowstone National Park in the USA, a wildfire burned for many months. It destroyed many of the park's pine forests and only went out when rain and snow fell. However, ten centimeters (four inches) of rain fell in 20 minutes, causing huge amounts of ash and mud to slip down mountainsides.

Can wildfires be predicted?

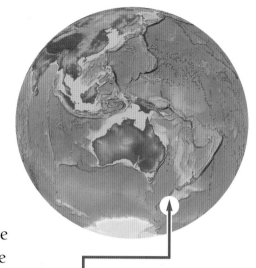

Saying that something will happen in the future is called making a prediction. Predicting a wildfire is impossible.

Certain types of weather will make it easier for a wildfire to start or keep burning. All that can be done is to watch the weather very closely during fire season. Weather scientists, called meteorologists, help the fire department decide if the fire danger is high, by letting them know if hot, dry, windy weather is expected. **Satellites** that spin around the Earth take pictures of the forests. Satellites can also measure how much water is inside the plants and trees. The satellite pictures show meteorologists if the vegetation is dry enough to burn.

Satellite pictures can show meteorologists and fire departments if the vegetation is dry or wet.

Fire restrictions

It is important for everyone to know what the fire danger is. Fire departments will put up signs along highways and at campsites at the beginning of the fire season in their area. These signs let everyone know how high the fire danger is.

During the fire danger period, special rules apply. These rules are called fire restrictions. When the fire danger is high, campfires or barbecues cannot be lit in an open space such as grassland or a forest. Anybody using farm machinery or hot welding torches must follow special safety instructions because sparks from their equipment can easily start a fire. The only fires allowed to burn are controlled fires lit by the fire department and those people who have permission to do so.

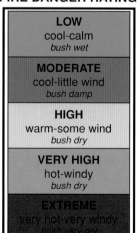

FIRE DANGER RATING

LOW
cool-calm
bush wet

MODERATE
cool-little wind
bush damp

HIGH
warm-some wind
bush dry

VERY HIGH
hot-windy
bush dry

EXTREME
very hot-very windy
bush very dry

Fire danger signs use colors as well as words to indicate how high the fire danger is. This is the fire danger sign used in New South Wales, Australia.

Total fire ban

A total fire ban means that nobody is allowed to light a fire at all. Total fire ban days are declared when the fire danger is extremely high. On these days, the weather conditions mean that a fire could develop quickly and be very difficult to control.

Anybody who does not obey the fire restrictions is breaking the law. Nobody wants to spoil the fun of summer; it is just a way of making sure that everyone is safer.

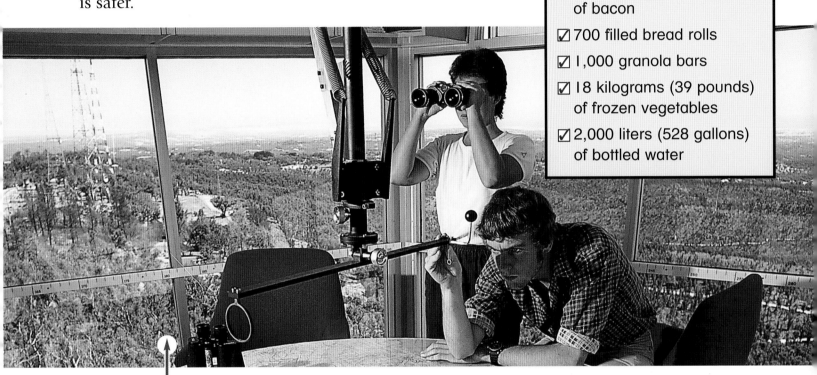

Fire spotters watch the forest for any sign of wildfire.

Fire spotters

During fire season, fire spotters are always looking out for wildfires. Fire towers have been built on the tops of hills to give fire spotters an excellent view of the countryside around them. Smoke can easily be spotted and reported by radio. When a large fire is blazing, all the towers may be occupied 24 hours a day.

Fire-spotting aircraft are flown over areas of thick forest. It is the quickest and easiest way to find a wildfire and work out how big the danger is. Before aircraft or fire towers were invented, some wildfires would go unnoticed because they burned in places where nobody lived.

How firefighters fight wildfires

Because most wildfires burn in places where they can do no harm to people, they are left to burn just as nature meant them to. Wildfires are only fought when they threaten lives and buildings. Firefighters are trained to control or put out wildfires. To do this, they must take away at least one of the three parts of the fire triangle: fuel, heat or oxygen.

Breaking the fire triangle

Removing fuel

Firefighters dig a shallow ditch called a **fire line** or fire break around the front of the fire. By clearing away leaves, branches and roots from the fire line, there is no fuel left to burn. Sometimes the firefighters will dig the fire line using a hand tool called a rakehoe. At other times, a bulldozer will do it for them. This is called dry firefighting because water is not being used to attack the fire.

A backing fire can also be lit inside the fire break. A backing fire burns towards the oncoming fire. It uses up all the fuel and both fires go out because there is nothing left to burn. This method is also called backburning.

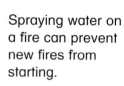

Spraying water on a fire can prevent new fires from starting.

Firefighters dig a fire line or fire break using heavy machinery. This is called dry firefighting.

Cooling

Water is sprayed on a fire to cool it down and to stop nearby fuel from preheating. People often protect their homes by spraying roofs and filling gutters with water so that hot embers cannot start new fires.

Limiting oxygen

Throwing dirt or pumping water on the flames stops the fire getting oxygen from the air. Without oxygen, it becomes too difficult for the fire to breathe.

Firefighting equipment

Tankers

Wildfires usually happen in places where there are few roads. Even if there is a track running through the forest, it is not always wide enough to take a fire tanker. Often, the firefighters must leave their vehicle and fight the fire on foot. They carry a small tank of water on their back like a backpack. It has a hose with a spray nozzle attached to it.

Fire tankers must have their own water supply.

There are some vehicles that are specially designed to drive through the forest. Instead of wheels they have tracks like a tank or a bulldozer. However, there is no water available in most wildfire areas. Once the water tank is empty firefighters have no way of refilling it unless there is a farm or house nearby.

An aircraft dumps water on the flames.

Aircraft and helicopters

Aircraft called water bombers drop huge amounts of water or **fire retardant** mixture onto the flames. Fire retardant contains a sticky chemical that smothers the fire. It also contains fertilizer to help the new plants grow after the flames have passed. The red color lets the pilot know where the retardant has been dropped.

Helicopters carry a huge bucket of water on a long cable. As the helicopter hovers over the fire, the bucket is emptied. A helicopter does not need to land on a runway like an airplane does. It can hover above dams, lakes and swimming pools and dip the bucket into the water to refill it.

If the water is too shallow for the bucket, another type of helicopter is used. It has a pipe that can be dropped into the water. The water is then pumped up into a tank inside the helicopter. The tank is opened as the helicopter passes over the wildfire.

Dressing for a fire

Firefighters can spend many hours fighting a wildfire. This means they must wear protective clothing that is specially designed for the job. Their bright yellow uniforms are made from material treated with a special chemical that resists burning and melting at high temperatures. This material is also light to help keep the firefighters cooler. Thick gloves are worn to protect their hands from the fire and from the sharp saw blades they use to cut down trees. A helmet is always worn to avoid injury from falling branches. Goggles and breathing equipment are used in places where smoke is thick.

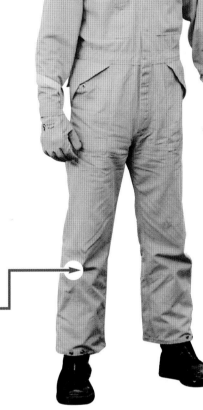

GUESS WHAT?

Most firefighters lose about 1.5 liters (more than two pints) of sweat during heavy work near a fire. Some have even lost as much as two liters (more than three pints).

Firefighters need special protective clothing to do their job safely.

Firefighting is dangerous work

Firefighters are very brave people. They have to work in extremely hot temperatures. They also work in heavy rain, through lightning storms and in darkness to help others and protect homes. Being near a fire means watching out for special dangers such as falling tree branches, loose rocks, and animals frightened by the **blaze**.

Firefighters must face choking smoke. Ash and soot can sting their eyes. They get very tired and thirsty—anyone who fights a fire must drink plenty of water. The intense heat of the flames can overheat the body. If firefighters sweat too much and drink too little they can even die.

GUESS WHAT?

In the USA, there are firefighters specially trained to fight fires in difficult places such as dense forest or mountain slopes. They are called smokejumpers. Smokejumpers parachute into the fire area from an aircraft. While they pack away their parachutes, the aircraft drops boxes of equipment and enough food and bottled water for three days.

Can wildfires be prevented?

Many wildfires are started by careless people. Others are lit on purpose. These wildfires can harm people; they often threaten towns and farms and cause millions of dollars of damage.

You can help prevent wildfires. Remember, everybody has a right to feel safe. It is okay to tell the person in charge if you see anyone behaving carelessly or playing with fire.

Protection from wildfire

When a wildfire spreads beyond the forest it can threaten homes and lives. As cities grow bigger, many people have to build their houses closer to natural bushland or forest areas. They may have little protection if a wildfire happens. In the past, some wildfires have even burned right to the edges of large cities.

Evacuation

When a wildfire approaches, some people may choose to leave the area and stay somewhere safe until the danger has passed. When people are moved to safety it is called evacuation. Those who want to stay and defend their homes should get advice from the fire department on how to best prepare for a wildfire.

Can you see why this house is not ready for the fire season?

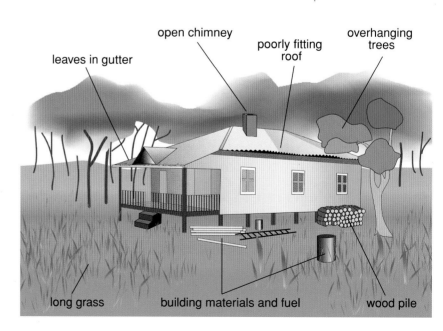

open chimney

poorly fitting roof

overhanging trees

leaves in gutter

long grass

building materials and fuel

wood pile

After the flames have gone

When the flaming front has passed, the fuel burns by glowing combustion. It is at this time that embers can be blown into gutters to start fresh spot fires. Or the wind may feed the embers extra oxygen, making the embers flare up into flames again. It is important for adults to look around and put out any small fires or **smoldering** fuel.

Mopping up

As well as putting out fires, firefighters have the long job of **mopping up**. Wherever the fire has burned, the firefighters must turn over every piece of wood to make sure that nothing is left alight. Smoking or glowing embers are covered with dirt or water.

Firefighters mopping up after a wildfire.

Read All About It!

Tasmania, Australia, 1967: In less than half a day, fires destroyed 2,000 buildings, 80 bridges, 1,500 vehicles, 5,000 power poles and 500 kilometers (312 miles) of power lines. Sixty-two people died, hundreds were injured and 3,000 were left homeless. On the farms, fires killed 50,000 sheep, 25,000 chickens, 1,400 cattle and 900 pigs.

Rebuilding

Wildfires can destroy entire towns. Many people evacuated during the emergency will return to find that they have no home. The only possessions they have left may be the few things they had time to grab before leaving.

Organizations such as the Red Cross and the Salvation Army provide food, clothes and a bed for those left homeless. Community shelters are set up in town halls or other large buildings that are undamaged by the fire.

Everybody helps after the wildfire. People give canned food, clothes and furniture. Many of the children will have lost all their toys and books. Special events are held to raise money to replace as many of these things as possible. However, even with all of this help and kindness, there will be many people who will spend a long time living in tents or caravans while they clear away the burnt wreckage of their homes. People can lose everything they own when a wildfire blazes through.

People can lose everything they own in a wildfire.

One of the relief centers set up after the Ash Wednesday wildfires in Australia, in 1983.

Studying wildfires

Scientists study wildfires. The information they learn is important because it can help make a firefighter's job easier and safer. It can also teach us how to better look after our forests as well as our own homes.

How fast will a wildfire spread? Which way will it travel? These are the questions the scientists are most interested in. Fire research units light controlled fires to see if it is possible to predict how a wildfire will behave. In a laboratory, they use wind tunnels to observe how hot embers travel on the wind. This is very important research because hot embers can start fresh fires up to 30 kilometers (18 miles) ahead of the main fire. Other scientists invent **fire-resistant** cloth so that firefighters will get better protection from the **radiant** heat of the flames.

To help them study wildfire behavior, Australian scientists lit 120 controlled grassfires in different weather and fuel conditions.

One of the newest developments is a **bushfire spread simulator**. When this specialized computer **software** is loaded on to a computer, it enables firefighters to work out where the wildfire is likely to spread and how best to fight it.

Record-breaking fires

The largest fire in the last 300 years

The Black Dragon fire

The Black Dragon fire began in China in 1987. It burned 1.2 million hectares (three million acres) of land and killed 220 people. It travelled north into Russia where it burned a further six million hectares (15 million acres).

One of the most costly fires

Yellowstone National Park, USA

Twenty-five thousand firefighters attended the fires in Yellowstone National Park. A total of US$120 million was spent in a desperate effort to stop the blaze.

The most disastrous fire in recent history

Peshtigo, USA

In 1871, a fierce, wind-driven fire swept through the town of Peshtigo, killing 1,500 people. People who rushed into the river and stood neck-deep in the water were among the few survivors.

The most area burned in a day

Yellowstone National Park, USA

The Yellowstone fires began burning in June, 1988. On August 20, 1988, hurricane-force wind gusts whipped up the flames and 66,000 hectares (165,000 acres) burned in just one day.

Glossary

ash	The black powder or flakes left behind after something has burned.
blaze	A large, fiercely burning fire.
bushfire spread simulator	A computer program that helps firefighters work out how quickly a fire might spread and in which direction it might travel.
canopy	The top part of the forest.
charred	Burned or turned into charcoal.
conduction	The movement of heat through something.
convection	The movement of heat through the air.
crown fire	A fire that burns the treetops in a forest.
ember	The glowing fuel left after the flames have passed.
fire line	A shallow ditch dug by firefighters to hold a fire. Also called a fire break.
fire-resistant	Will not easily catch on fire or burn.
fire retardant	Something that slows a fire down.
fire triangle	The three things needed for a fire to burn: fuel, heat and oxygen.
flaming front	The burning edge of the fire.
glowing combustion	When a fire burns slowly without a flame.
ignition point	The temperature at which fuel begins to burn.
indigenous peoples	People who are the original occupants of an area.
intense	Extremely strong or hot.
monsoon	Winds that blow from the sea, bringing almost constant heavy rain.
mopping up	Making sure that no fuel still burns by glowing combustion.
predator	An animal that eats another animal.
preheating	The time when a fuel is heating up but is below its ignition point.
radiant	Moving out from a center (or source) in rays or waves.
radiation	When heat moves in waves or rays from a heat source.
reaction	A change that happens when two or more chemicals are mixed together.
satellite	A small spacecraft above the Earth that sends back information about the weather.
smoldering	Burning slowly and producing smoke but no flames.
software	A set of instructions that tells a computer how to do certain things.
superheating	Heating something to an extremely high temperature.
thrive	To grow strongly and quickly.
understory	The plants that grow beneath the canopy, or treetops, of a forest.
vegetation	The trees, plants and grasses in a particular area.

Index

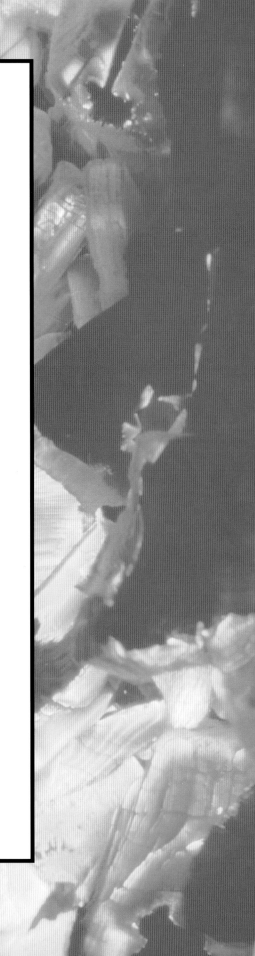